IGNITING FAITH IN 40 DAYS

by
Steve & Wendy Backlund

****

ISBN 978-1-59872-758-6

****

Many thanks to the following for their input in the writ
devotionals: Elaine Smith, Dale Kaz, Jeanie Sanda
Alderson, and Maureen Puddle.

****

This book is dedicated to:
our children -
Joel, Kyle, and Heidi

We also dedicate this book to the congregations at
Desert Oasis Christian Center
in Round Mountain, Nevada, and
Mountain Chapel in Weaverville,
California. Thanks for loving us,
pouring into us, and believing in us
as we have sought to be all that God
has called us to be.

Finally, we also dedicate this book
to Bill Johnson and Kris Vallotton.
Thank you for following your dream
and paying a price so we could find
God and His goodness in a way we
never thought we could.

Table of Contents

Introduction

I invite you on a forty day journey to change the way you think. Transformation starts with our thoughts (Romans 12:1,2). The quality of our lives and the advancement of God's kingdom depend on "renewing the spirit of our minds" (Eph 4:22-24).

Wendy and I have learned that true faith is built on hope; a confident, optimistic expectation about the future based on God's promises & a revelation of His goodness. This book is filled with hope for you, your family, your church, your city, & your nation.

Get ready to grow. Get ready to declare God's promises. Get ready for transformation. Today is the first day of the rest of your life. We bless you as you Ignite Your Faith.

Steve Backlund

How to Use This Book

*Igniting Faith in 40 Days** has two major components. The first is the daily devotional teaching which will strengthen you through its biblical principles of faith. The second is the speaking forth of the declarations mentioned in #2 and #3 below - "faith comes by hearing . . ." (Rom 10:17). Even though there is benefit in just reading this book, consider this radical format to maximize its contents:

1. **Read** a teaching (devotional) each day for 40 days
2. **Boldly speak** the declaration for the devotiona
3. **Boldly speak** one of the declaration lists from the back of the book (do both morning and night)
4. **Read** Mark, Galatians, Proverbs, and chapter 4 from Romans, Philippians, and Hebrews during the 40 days.
5. **Listen** to one or all of these CD series during the 40 days: Relentless Mind Renewal, Victorious Faith, or Framing Our Future. Available at ignitedhope.com
6. **Go** on a **"negativity fast"** during the 40 days. This book is an ideal resource to use during this kind of fast. Helps for your negativy fast are available in the appendix in the back of the book.
7. **Finally**, and most important, **find one or more others to join you in this experience**

* the message of this book is not a single formula of success, but a necessary ingredient to add to a life of intimacy with Jesus.

Use the **checklist** that is on most pages to help you.
The abbreviations of the checklist are:
- BR (Bible reading)
- RD (read devotional)
- DD (spoke devotional declaration)
- OD (other declarations spoken from back of book)
- NF (negativity fast)

Day #1

Legal vs. Experiential Ownership

Every place . . . I have given you (Joshua 1:3)

Joshua chapter one is the place to go for those ready to leave "wilderness Christianity." Joshua was called to lead the new generation into the Promised Land. In verse two, God says, "Go to the land I am giving you." He adds in verse three, "Every place your foot treads, I have given you." Then verse four gives the boundaries to what was theirs.

It's fascinating that they are told what is legally theirs before they experientially possessed it. Legal ownership was no guarantee of experiential ownership. It was called the Promised Land so they would confidently proceed to possess it - no matter what obstacles they encountered.

It is no different for us today. We have our own "promised land." It's not a geographical area, but it is specific blessings. For instance, every person has the legal ownership of eternal life, but that must be possessed experientially through faith in Christ. Also, God promises us health, favor, spiritual power, protection, abundant provision, wisdom, and much more. Peter refers to the "exceedingly, great and precious promises" which were given to us "to participate in the divine nature" (2 Peter 1:4). We may have to overcome many challenges to experience these promises, but we can. Let's persevere and keep seeking to possess what is already legally ours.

Declare: I am what the Bible says I am. I have what it says I have. I can do what it says I can do. I increasingly possess in my experience the promises of God.

Checklist to Ignite Your Faith: ___ BR, ___ RD, ___ DD, ___OD, ___ NF.

The abbreviations are: BR (Bible reading), RD (read devotional), DD (declared devotional declaration), OD (other declarations spoken from back of book), NF (negativity fast).

Day #2
A Lying Apple Tree?
Calling those things that are not . . . **(Romans 4:17)**

An apple tree will produce apples because of what it is. When it is young, it will have no apples; but it still must say, "I am an apple tree." When it is winter and there are no leaves or apples; it still says, "I am an apple tree." Is it lying at those times? No. It would be lying to say anything different.

Many Christians have a hard time saying who God says they are when no fruit is manifesting in that particular area. Could they be "too young" in that truth to be fruitful? Could they be in a season where that dimension of the Christian life is being pruned back for future growth? Either way, it does not mean they are lying when they say, "I am anointed, prosperous, delivered, healed, righteous, strong etc."

Joel 3:10 says, "Let the weak say I am strong." We don't deny the fact of weakness, but we focus on the greater truth that we are strong in Him.

Again, because the Word says we ARE these things, we would be untruthful to say anything different. Let's not lie against the truth. Indeed we ARE what the Bible says we are.

Declare: I am who the Word says I am. I have a sound mind. I have great favor with God and man. People love me. I am a happy person. I love life and enjoy every day. I am healed. I have abundant provision. I am blessed and protected. I increasingly know who and what I am in Christ. I make a tremendous difference for Christ wherever I go.

Checklist to Ignite Faith ___ BR, ___ RD, ___ DD, ___OD, ___ NF.

Check out ignitedhope.com and find extra insight concerning the power of declarations. Click on "declarations" at the site.

Day #3

Bringing Life to Dead Places
Let the weak say "I am strong" (Joel 3:10)

God has called us to make "dead things" alive. In Ezekiel 37, the prophet was asked if the dry bones could live. In the dialogue and events that followed, God showed Ezekiel and His people a powerful principle that is vital for us today.

God's method of bringing life to these "very dry" bones was through Ezekiel prophesying "life" to the whole situation. Ezekiel had to speak to the bones. He had to prophesy to the wind. As he did, things changed and life came.

You and I also must continually speak to dead areas in our lives and circumstances. A main "method" of God bringing change to a situation is for one of His children to speak His promises over people and circumstances. "And God who gives life to the dead and calls those things that are not as though they are" (Romans 4:17).

It starts with each of us prophesying "life" over ourselves. Joel gives us a good place to start in Joel 3:10, "Let the weak say I am strong." Start now a life long habit to "call those things that are not as though they are" in your life.

Declare: Even though I feel weak at times, I am really strong. I am very strong to accomplish God's purpose in my life and to be a strength to others. I prophesy daily over my circumstances, my future, and over the dry areas of my life.

Checklist to Ignite Faith ___ BR, ___ RD, ___ DD, ___OD, ___ NF.

> If you don't understand something written in this book, just set that aside and continue on your journey. Most things will be clarified in the 40 days.

Day #4
Praying in Faith (Part I)
Mary has chosen the best part (Luke 10:42)

Often people spend much effort and time praying over a circumstance hoping that *time and quantity* of prayer will bring the desired result. The hope is that perhaps faith will increase through this effort and thus the prayer will be answered.

This kind of thinking implies that faith is built by the amount of time and energy expended. We need to understand that faith does not come through our effort. Faith is a result of what we "know." Our "measure of faith" (Romans 12:3) will increase in proportion to the revelation we have of God's character, His love, and His promises toward us.

Often we do not realize the value of spending time with God when we are not praying for needs. The reason we worship, quietly wait in His presence, and search the scripture is mainly to build a relationship and to learn about the character, power, and love of God. Our intimacy and relationship with Him will have a direct correlation to our level of faith; not because it "earns" us more authority, but because it gives something for our faith to stand on.

Declare: My trust and faith in God grows in the proportion to how much I know His character, goodness, and trustworthiness. I therefore spend much time in His presence developing intimacy with Him.

Checklist to Ignite Faith ___ BR, ___ RD, ___ DD, ___OD, ___ NF.

Never become satisfied with a mere theology of God's presence in your private life or church life. Pursue His manifested presence!

Day #5
Praying in Faith (Part 2)
Prayer . . . avails much (James 5:16)

As we battle spiritual forces, it is important to distinguish between the burden of the Lord and the weight of unbelief. We must take inventory of our emotions as we pray. Is a spirit of fear, anxiety, or hopelessness present? Do we feel "under the circumstance" that we are praying about? Are we consistently begging for God's help? If so, the heaviness we are feeling is probably not about the circumstance we are facing, but from our own beliefs about God and life.

These emotions are not going to go away just by praying longer, fasting, or praying harder. We also cannot pretend these emotions are not there. We need to confront them and rebuke spirits of unbelief, fear, and hopelessness. We can start this by repenting of wrong core beliefs that hinder confidence in the power of our prayers. Then we must turn our eyes to God's faithfulness and worship Jesus until we get a revelation of His goodness and love toward us. **The battle is first in us and then in our circumstances.**

Declare: Fear and doubt are my main enemies. I am not a victim to these emotions. I replace the lies fueling them with the promises of God. I trust in the goodness of God.

Checklist to Ignite Faith ___ BR, ___ RD, ___ DD, ___OD, ___ NF.

"Spirits of heaviness" in private or corporate prayer result from seeing the problem as bigger than God. Stir up God's promises before praying.

Day #6
Dealing with Uncertainty
Do not be anxious about anything (Phil 4:6)

2 Peter 1:4 says God's great promises empower us to "participate in the divine nature and escape the corruption that is in the world through lust." What a statement about the power of promises!

Here are five promises to get into your spirit to "blast away" uncertainty about the future:

> **I Can** - Philippians 4:13 says, "I can do all things through Christ who strengthens me." Whatever is needed from me, I can do it.
>
> **There is a Way** - I Corinthians 10:13 reveals there is a way for every person (whether to get out of a tough time or to get into God's purpose).
>
> **I've Prayed** - James 5:16,17 tells us that our prayers are powerful and effective. Things will be different because we pray.
>
> **God Will Finish What He Has Started** - Philippians 1:6 tells us to be confident of God's finishing power.
>
> **It Will Be OK** - Romans 8:28 says that all things will work for good in my life as I focus on two things: 1) God's call for me, and 2) loving Jesus Christ first in my life.

Declare: God's exceedingly great and precious promises help me to wage war in my mind against lies about the future. I therefore cannot be defeated in Jesus' name. I am more than a conqueror.

Checklist to Ignite Faith ___ BR, ___ RD, ___ DD, ___OD, ___ NF.

Day #7
Cut Off From Grace
. . . miracles . . . by the hearing of faith? (Gal 3:5)

"Does God supply His Spirit and work miracles among you by the works of the law or by the hearing of faith?" (Galatians 3:5). This is probably the second most important question in the Bible. [Only "Who do you say I (Jesus) am?" would be more important.] The Apostle Paul asks this penetrating question in the book of Galatians, which is a "must read" and "must study" for the advancing saint. He was rebuking those in Galatia for returning to a performance-based religion - instead of keeping a "faith based relationship." It is a strong book with strong words such as, "You who seek to be justified by the law have been cut off from grace" (Galatians 5:4).

Grace is the empowerment to do God's will. Most people probably think that persistence in sin leads to a cutting off of grace's flow; but, in reality, we are cut off from God's power when we believe that God is more concerned with our behavior than He is with our beliefs.

Here's a truth that will keep us in grace: What is believed about something is more important than what is done about it. Good works are important, but they primarily result from a proper "belief system" in our lives.

Declare: I reject a works-based Christianity. I declare I have faith to receive all of God's blessings and His empowerment to change my life and the world. I now receive a new measure of grace through faith.

Checklist to Ignite Faith ___ BR, ___ RD, ___ DD, ___OD, ___ NF.

Day #8

Rose Colored Glasses

. . through . . . Scriptures . . . might have hope (Ro 15:4)

Sometimes optimistic people are accused of seeing life through "rose colored" glasses. Their vision supposedly is affected by an unrealistic perspective that blinds them to life's negatives and accentuates only the positives.

All Christians have predispositions that influence how the Bible is interpreted, and thus how life is viewed. These unconscious inclinations are often influenced by the "traditions of men" which limit positive expectancy for the future (see Mark 7:13).

Romans 15:4 tells us that hope results from proper Bible "learning." Later in verse 13 we are told that joy, peace, and abounding hope come from "believing." There should be a corresponding increase of hope in our lives that is proportional to the amount of the Bible we consume.

Unfortunately, many church teachings limit hope. For example, most "end times" teachings decrease positive expectation for lives, families, cities, and the nations of the world. As a result, many don't live with hope and faith because of a predisposition that believes "the world is getting worse" (and not better). This hopelessness indicates we need an alteration in our interpretation of Scripture. Truly, hope grows with each encounter with God's Word and with the God of hope.

Declare: I see the Bible and life through "blood colored" glasses. I therefore abound in hope for my life and for everyone connected to me. God's promises are true. My prayers are powerful and effective. My hope helps release God's kingdom in our midst.

Checklist to Ignite Faith ___ BR, ___ RD, ___ DD, ___OD, ___ NF.

Who Do You Think You Are! (Part 1)
. . . but your name shall be called Abraham (Gen. 17:5)

Abram received a promise that his descendents would be as numerous as the stars and the sand of the seashore. The problem was that he was very old, and his wife was past childbearing years and had been barren all of her life. The prophetic word concerning his innumerable descendents was laughable to the "landlocked" mind.

Well, after more than two decades of no manifestation of the promise, it seemed even more impossible. Although Abram's faith grew, there was still no baby for Sarah and him.

Finally, at 100 years old, they had their promised son, Isaac (which means laughter). What made the difference? The key change was this: Abram's name was changed to Abraham - which means "father of a multitude." As Abram called himself by the promises of God, "he was strengthened in faith" and saw the promise come to pass. (See Romans 4 for insight on this process.)

So who do you think you are? Is your identity shaped by your past or by the promises of God? Your answer will largely determine whether God's "laughable promises" over your life will come to pass.

Declare: I am who God says I am. I can do what He says I can do. I will see His promises come to pass in me as I speak His promises over my life.

Checklist to Ignite Faith ___ BR, ___ RD, ___ DD, ___OD, ___ NF.

We won't have it just because we say it,
but saying it is a big part of having it.

Day #10

Who Do You Think You Are! (Part 2)
Calling those things that are not, as though they were (Romans 4:17)

Here is a major life question: Does our experience create our identity or does our identity create our experience? The answer is . . . (drum roll please) . . . our identity creates our experience. Remember, those who think they can, and those who think they can't, are both right (consider the spies in Numbers 13 and 14). What we believe about ourselves will either bind us or launch us.

When it comes to who we think we are, God is calling us to believe His Word instead of negative experiences. He says "Consider yourselves dead to sin, but alive to God . . . " (Romans 6:11), and "Let the weak say I am strong" (Joel 3:10). Abraham "did not consider his own body, already dead . . ." (Romans 4:19).

Satan, on the other hand, wants us to focus on our failures and lack. A battle rages in our souls concerning what to believe about ourselves. Do we "call ourselves" by our negative experience or by God's promise. Proverbs 23:7 declares "As (a man) thinks in his heart, so is he." Let's think God's thoughts about us, and not anything else.

Declare: I am a new creation in Christ. Old things have passed away. All things are new. I am strong in Christ. I am who the Bible says I am.

Checklist to Ignite Faith ___ BR, ___ RD, ___ DD, ___OD, ___ NF.

As a man thinks in his heart so is he.

Day #11
Non-Negotiable Convictions
Daniel . . . three times a day . . . prayed . . . as was his custom since his early days (Dan 6:10)

Daniel was a man of conviction. Even the threat of the lion's den did not move him away from his godly habits. He built his life around life-producing priorities. In great contrast, the prophet Malachi rebuked the people of his day for giving their "leftovers" to the Lord (see Malachi chapter one). Unlike Daniel, God had become a burden to them, rather than a delight.

Two things cause convictions that burn in our hearts and which become non-negotiable: 1) loving God's presence, and 2) a strong vision for the future. Without these, we will only give God our leftovers.

Here are areas for your convictions to develop in: time with God and His Word, fellowship and worship, serving in ministry, financial giving, speaking God's promises, prioritizing our family, having strong accountability relationships, and putting ourselves in places where God's power can touch our lives and the lives of others.

Like Daniel, do you have spiritual non-negotiable convictions? Or are you fighting the "leftover battle" as the people in Malachi's day? Today is the first day of the rest of your life. Build your schedule around God's priorities like never before. You won't be sorry.

Declare: I give God the first portion of my life and He takes care of all my needs. I am a person of conviction. I have dominion over my life and my time. I burn with a personal vision that leads me to sacrifice for God and His presence.

Checklist to Ignite Faith ___ BR, ___ RD, ___ DD, ___OD, ___ NF.

Day #12

Do Not Say . . .

Do not say I am only a youth (Jeremiah 1:7)

Has anyone ever told you, "Don't say that"? Probably. (We've all been guilty of speaking something we shouldn't have.) Well, Jeremiah experienced someone "calling him" on what he said. That someone happened to be God. He challenged Jeremiah's self-restricting statement, "I am only a youth."

God had already told him, "Before you were born . . . I ordained you a prophet to the nations." Jeremiah however focused on his apparent limitations rather than on the word of the Lord. He uttered an "I can't do that" proclamation that many in the church today would have applauded as true humility. God said though, "Do not say that."

Remember, those that say "I can" and those who say "I can't" are both right. Now is the time for us to take another look at what we speak, especially when we declare what we think we cannot do. Our words are either a rudder to direct our lives into God's prophetic will (James 3:5) or a curse that puts fences around our potential.

We must believe before we see (not the other way around). One of the main truths we are to believe is Philippians 4:13, "I can do all things through Christ . . ."

Declare: I renounce every curse I have spoken over my life through declarations of what I thought I could not do. I will not limit God, but will release Him by joining the Apostle Paul's positive declaration in saying "I CAN!"

Checklist to Ignite Faith ___ BR, ___ RD, ___ DD, ___OD, ___ NF.

> Weightlifters build muscles by pressing against resistance. Faith muscle is increased the same way by pressing against old thought patterns.

Day #13

Where Am I

Out of the abundance of the heart the mouth speaks
(Matt 12:33)

If you want to know where you are and where you are going in your spiritual life, listen to your own words. Jesus said, "Out of the abundance of the heart the mouth speaks. A good man out of the good treasure of his heart brings forth good things, and an evil man out of the evil treasure brings forth evil things" (Matthew 12:33-34). He then adds that, on the day of judgment, we will give an account for every "idle" word we speak (verse 35).

The word "treasure" in verse 34 could be translated "deposit"; thus, whatever has been deposited in our lives will come out in words. Our words are powerful forces that not only reveal our spiritual condition; but also dynamically impact our future and that of others. This is why we will have to answer for every idle (non-life producing) word we speak.

Where are we? Our words are our indicator - especially words spoken when we are under pressure. Where are we going? Like a ship's rudder, our words will direct our destiny (James 3:4,5). What then do we need to do? Radically make good deposits through thinking about and speaking God's truths. How do we know if we are ready for the next level in God? It's when our words consistently speak faith, hope, and love in the level we are in now.

Declare: My mouth is a powerful instrument for God's kingdom. I daily make good deposits into my heart. My words increasingly reveal a heart full of faith, a heart full of hope, and a heart full of love.

Checklist to Ignite Faith ___ BR, ___ RD, ___ DD, ___OD, ___ NF.

If we radically change our words about God and ourselves, we will find a shortcut through the wilderness of life.

Day #14
Kratos Power
The word of God grew mightily & prevailed (Acts 19:20)

There are three main Greek words for power in the New Testament. The first is dunamis - an explosive, "dynamite" power (Acts 1:8). The second is exousia - a power based on authority (John 1:12). Dunamis is as the policeman's gun, while exousia is the badge. The third "power word" is kratos - a societal transforming power (Acts 19:20 - "the word of God grew mightily and prevailed"). Dunamis and exousia manifest mostly in meetings, intercessory prayer, and in personal ministry. Kratos is an inner attitude of faith that "holds" a family, church, region, or nation in increasing blessings (the word "grew").

Elijah walked in kratos power when his prayer caused a three year drought. This happened because he practiced a powerful prayer truth: what is believed after prayer is just as important as what is believed during prayer. Elijah's kratos faith continued after the "prayer meeting." Romans 16:20 says, "The God of peace will soon crush Satan under your feet." As we mix God's word with faith, we will experience growing inner peace. This increasing peace lets us know that the manifestation of Satan's "crushing" is drawing near. Philippians 4:6,7 also speaks to this when we are commanded not to worry about anything, but to pray about everything with THANKSGIVING. It's this on-going thanksgiving that helps produce a kratos power - this inner attitude of faith that holds us in increasing blessing. When we water yesterday's prayers with thanksgiving today, we build up an "Elijah kind of prayer" that avails much.

Declare: I radically thank God for the prayers I prayed yesterday. I am thus growing in peace and kratos power that helps hold my life and others in the increasing blessing of God.

Checklist to Ignite Faith ___ BR, ___ RD, ___ DD, ___OD, ___ NF.

Day #15

Never Enough?

. . . works . . . or the hearing of faith (Galatians 3:2,5)

The devil wants us to believe that we are not doing enough to see revival happen. "If you do a little more," he says, "then it will really happen." He wants us to think that we are constantly falling short. He tempts us to focus more on *doing* than on *believing*.

"There isn't enough unity for revival."

"People aren't praying enough."

"You should have fasted one more day."

"You haven't gone long enough without sinning in that area."

We must resist the temptation to think that these fruits of revival are the cause of revival. If we don't, we will believe we are not ready or deserving of a continual outpouring. This negative belief can actually be a main blockage to our revival experience.

Again, many say, "Breakthrough and revival are 'just around the corner.' We're close, but . . . " Someone must respond to this by saying, "No! Revival began on the day of Pentecost in Acts 2. It's not about working more for it, but it's about believing that Jesus has already done everything that we could never do. He's done enough! Let us by faith release the manifestation of revival now!"

Declare: I am walking in personal revival. It's already here and I have chosen to believe it. I have received this outpouring from God by faith, not by works. As I believe, my life is propelled to prayer, to unity with others, to personal obedience and to sacrifice for kingdom advancement.

Checklist to Ignite Faith ___ BR, ___ RD, ___ DD, ___OD, ___ NF.

Day #16
End Times Theology
The gospel of the kingdom . . . **(Matthew 24:14)**

What do you believe about the end times? Will there be revival or will the world "go to hell in a hand basket" before Jesus returns? Will the church limp into heaven or will she have "made herself ready" and become the bride "without spot or wrinkle"? Our answers are crucial.

Matthew 24:14 says that the "gospel of the kingdom will be preached in every nation" before the end. Scripturally, the kingdom gospel demonstrates power with signs and wonders following. That does not sound like a weak church in the last hour.

One obstacle to having a victorious end time mind-set is that theologians seem to place most of the Bible's positive last days' promises in the millennium. End times books reinforce this mind-set; thus, our responsibility and expectation for kingdom advancement is diminished.

Consider this question: If a prophecy of judgment is given against a certain place, should Christians run to or run from that place? It would seem that biblical promises and commands would say, "Go and be salt. Preserve this place. Your presence will withhold devastation, save the people and make the difference." Why don't we think this way more? Could it be that we are believing incorrectly about the end times?

Declare: The church is triumphant. The end time church will be a "revival church" full of power and Christ likeness.

Checklist to Ignite Faith ___ BR, ___ RD, ___ DD, ___OD, ___ NF.

Our expectancy largely creates our future.
Expectancy is simply another word for faith.

Remember Your Benefits
Forget not all His benefits (Psalms 103:2)

Imagine an employee being ignorant of the benefits in his compensation package. What would you think if he pays for all his medical bills, but has health insurance? He would be either ignorant or unintelligent. Unfortunately, we as the people of God often do this in our spiritual lives.

The Psalmist says, "Bless the Lord, oh my soul, and forget not all His benefits, who forgives all your iniquities, who heals all your diseases . . ." (Psalms 103:2,3). We are instructed to deliberately remember what is in our "salvation package." The obvious implication is this: If we don't, we will believe we have to pay for things that have already been given to us.

We can't forget what we never knew. Some Christians are unaware that healing and other benefits are part of our salvation. The Greek word *sozo* is translated "to save" in the New Testament; but it also means to heal, to deliver, and to be made whole. It is refreshing that now there is a growing understanding that healing and transforming forgiveness are still benefits for the Christian, and are not just occasional sovereign blessings.

"Not forgetting" is more than a onetime event, but a "life long contending" for God's total benefit package for mankind. Truly, let's tell our soul to bless God and to radically remember how good He really is.

Declare: God is continually revealing to me my benefits as a Christian. I contend for these in my soul; and, thus, experience them more and more in my life.

Checklist to Ignite Faith ___ BR, ___ RD, ___ DD, ___OD, ___ NF.

Day #18
Presumptuous Faith
Abraham . . . was strengthened in faith (Rom. 4:20)

There are two common areas where "presumptuous faith" occurs. The first is when we make "faith decisions" exclusively through someone else's revelation (i.e. refusing medical treatment "by faith" because of another's testimony). The second can happen when we believe for a very specific, personal blessing (i.e. receiving that promotion, marrying so & so, having God providing for or vindicating us in **that** way, etc.).

Presumptuous faith is grounded more on our emotions than on God's word. It can be avoided by remembering these three important things:

1. **Build hope before "claiming" something specific by faith** – Hope is a general, abounding optimism concerning the future. A positive stronghold of hope decreases the likelihood that we will believe that God can only meet our need in one way.

2. **Strengthen faith by believing for small things** – Presumptuous people want to express a $1,000,000 faith when they have not even used their faith on the $100 level.

3. **Walk with others concerning faith** – Stay away from cynics and doubters, but do find people who can help discern presumption from real faith. Also, trust God to use spiritual mentors in clarifying His will and His voice.

Declare: I am strengthened in faith daily. My belief system is built on a solid foundation of hope. I am protected from presumptuous faith by hope, wisdom, and powerful people in my life.

Checklist to Ignite Faith ___ BR, ___ RD, ___ DD, ___OD, ___ NF.

Repenting From or Repenting To
Repent, for the kingdom of heaven is at hand (Matt 4:17)

A good definition of repentance is to "change the mind." The prefix "re-" means "again, anew, back or backward." "Pent" is the highest place - as in penthouse. Repentance therefore could be defined as "going back to the highest place of thinking."

Repentance is more than feeling sorry for the wrong things we have done. It is much more than seeking forgiveness and purposing to not sin again. It is important to repent 'to' something, not just 'from' something. It involves changing the mind from one course into a higher course.

We can "cry our eyes out" and not repent. True repentance is a decision to "take every thought captive to the obedience of Christ" (2 Corinthians 10:5). It's not just a defensive reaction, but it is an offensive plan that moves God's kingdom from "being at hand" to becoming a reality in our experience.

The kingdom of heaven is God's abundant life of salvation, peace, power, evangelism, integrity, purity, miracles, strong families, health, prosperity, blessings and more. We are commanded to pray "thy kingdom come, thy will be done; on earth as it is in heaven." This is God's highest place for His people. Our repenting creates an expectation that these will manifest; and this faith pulls them into our experience and those of others. Praise God! Let's take our repenting to a new level today.

Declare: I capture my thoughts and take them to God's highest place. I repent TO my "promise land" and not just FROM Egypt. I keep repenting daily by joyfully speaking God's promises over my life.

Checklist to Ignite Faith ___ BR, ___ RD, ___ DD, ___OD, ___ NF.

Day #20
Saints or Sinners
Paul . . . to the saints in Ephesus **(Ephesians 1:1)**

As Christians, are we saints or sinners? The answer is crucial. If we misdiagnose ourselves and other Christians, it will have dire consequences.

The Bible says that we are saints. Our conversion changed our identity. Some would say that this is only a matter of words. It's not. What we call ourselves is vital to walking in God's fullness.

A main reason Christians continue sinning is because they believe that is who they are. Instead, we are to believe we are dead to sin and alive to God who will cause us to make good choices (Romans 6:11-13). As we do, we will see obedience grow in our lives. Our experience will always "catch up" to what we truly believe.

Christian leaders also need to see their "flocks" as saints. If we believe we are leading sinners, then control and fear will dominate our leadership. If the people are seen as saints, then empowerment and positive expectation will reign (which will bring out the best in those being led).

As always, the true test in this comes when there is a failure. Do we allow the failure to strengthen the negative stronghold of "sinnerhood"; or do we challenge it and say, "There may have been sin, but that is not our true identity"?

Declare: I am a saint. I am prone to doing things right. I see other Christians as saints also. I will see increased obedience in my life and in the lives of those I influence.

Checklist to Ignite Faith ___ BR, ___ RD, ___ DD, ___OD, ___ NF.

We must recognize what God has put in us, before we will be able to release and expend it.

Something Greater Than Character
Now hope does not disappoint **(Romans 5:5)**

Romans 5:3-4 gives a tremendous road map for break-through. "We also glory in our tribulations, knowing that tribulation produces perseverance; and perseverance, character; and character, hope." Character would seem as a final goal for the Christian, but there is something beyond character that must be possessed; it's hope.

Hope is the confident expectation of good coming. It joins faith and love as the "big three" of Christianity (I Corinthians 13:13). Romans 15:13 says, "Now may the God of hope fill you with all joy and peace in believing, that you may abound in hope by the power of the Holy Spirit." This abounding hope is our goal.

Biblical hope is radical optimism for us, others, our family, the church, our communities, and beyond. This positive expectation releases God's promises in a way that character never could (for kingdom life does not manifest because of good works but by our faith). Godly character cannot be bypassed, but there is something more (hope) that is truly needed to impact the world in exponential ways.

Declare: My future is as bright as the promises of God. I therefore am a person of abounding hope. I expect God's goodness to increase daily in my life and surroundings.

Checklist to Ignite Faith ___ BR, ___ RD, ___ DD, ___OD, ___ NF.

When we are fearful, we have too much faith
in Satan and not enough in God. Fear is
confidence in something bad happening.

Day #22
The Crucial Moment
Taking every thought captive **(2 Corinthians 10:5)**

What are the most important moments in the life of a growing Christian? Is it a powerful "God encounter"? Is it a fresh dedication to the purposes of God? Is it when we hear "what the spirit is saying to the church?"

While these are important, I propose that there is another "God moment" that will have a greater effect on our destiny than these. What is it? It's when we fail or have experiences that do not line up with the promises of God.

In that moment, we have a choice. Do we keep our identity (and God's identity) in His promises or do we use experience to empower a negative identity for us and God? We must remember that negative strongholds are created and strengthened when we put our experiences above God's Word.

When failure happens, we must think like this: "I may have sinned, but I am not a sinner. I may have had an accident, but I have a covenant of protection. I may be experiencing lack, but I am a prosperous person. Healing may not have manifested, but I am healed and I bring healing to others." Yes, I may need to get help from others concerning the failure, but I resist the temptation to make negative conclusions.

Those who passively rely on experience to identify who they are (and who God is) will greatly limit God in their lives. However, those who seize these crucial moments by taking thoughts captive will powerfully break down restrictive strongholds and enter into their "promise land."

Declare: I rejoice in apparent times of failure. These are my crucial moments in life. I declare once more that I am who the Bible says I am.

Checklist to Ignite Faith ___ BR, ___ RD, ___ DD, ___OD, ___ NF.

Day #23

Faith Makes a Difference
Your faith has made you well (Mark 5:34)

The book of Mark reveals the power of faith in the individual's life:
- "When Jesus saw **their faith**, He (forgave and healed)" - Mark 2:5
- "Daughter, **your faith** has made you well" - 5:34
- "If you can believe, all things are possible to **him who believes**" - 9:23.
- "Go your way, **your faith** has made you well" 10:52
- "Have faith in God . . . whoever says to this mountain, 'be removed' . . . and does not doubt . . . but **believes** . . . he will have whatever he says . . . whatever things you ask when you pray, believe that you receive them, and you will have them" - 11:22-24

God's full salvation is released by faith. It is also restricted by unbelief (see Mark 6 where Jesus was limited by the lack of faith in Nazareth, and look also at Mark 4:40; 9:19).

A major turning point in the Christian life is this: having the belief that our faith makes a difference in what we and our descendents experience in health, prosperity, mental clarity, ministry effectiveness, longevity of life, blessings, and protection; and believing that our unbelief will restrict the flow of these kingdom benefits. Surely these thoughts must be understood in cooperation with other important truths; but we must believe our faith (or our unbelief) makes a difference, or we will live far below God's highest will for our lives.

Declare: Like Abraham, I am strengthened in faith daily. Kingdom advancement and kingdom benefits are increasingly being released in my life because of my faith. I am a "difference maker" for everyone in my life, both now and after I leave planet earth.

Day #24

Walking Off a Two Story Spiritual Roof
Meditate on this book of the law day and night (Josh 1:8)

Can you imagine someone walking off a two-story roof, breaking his leg and then blaming God for what happened? That would be ridiculous. Well, that is in essence what some do by ignoring the laws of the spirit.

Law is "a scientific fact or phenomenon that is unchanged under given conditions" (Encarta World English Dictionary). The law of gravity is an example of this. It needs to be understood and allowed to control every day decisions or there could be serious consequences!

It is also foolish to not live by spiritual laws - which are just as real and also must be grasped and applied. Scripture speaks of these "laws" or spiritual principles that ultimately control the natural dimension that we live in. It is important that we understand that there are truths to be esteemed for safe and successful living (whether it is the law of honor, honesty, sexual purity, agreement, sowing and reaping, tithing, faith, or speaking life). Only a fool would think that our choices, thoughts, and words have no consequences.

So, are you walking off a two-story roof in the spirit realm, thinking you can defy the laws of the spirit? It won't work. You'll get hurt. Cry out now for the heavenly wisdom to know what is real and true. You won't be sorry. You'll be blessed.

Declare: I love God's laws. They are revealed to me daily. Through Jesus I walk in the laws of God.

Checklist to Ignite Faith ___ BR, ___ RD, ___ DD, ___OD, ___ NF.

We often think we need to hold on to feelings of guilt
to keep ourselves "in check", rather than embrace
a new identity that will produce "new fruit."

Walking Off a Two Story Spiritual Roof (Part 2)
Meditate on this book of the law day and night (Josh 1:8)

The law of gravity can either work for us or against us. Stepping off a cliff will cause pain, but water descending at a dam will produce power. One "law" makes both happen. Gravity can help us or hurt us.

The laws of the spirit also work for us or against us. Wisdom is using them for powerful results. Foolishness is violating these laws. Just as life's natural laws are "no respecter of person", neither are the laws of the spirit realm. "God is not mocked. A man reaps what he sows" (Galatians 6:7). Hosea said, "My people are destroyed for lack of knowledge" (4:6). Truly, there is destruction when we don't have the wisdom of God's laws guiding our lives.

God has not destined us to destruction, but ordained us to release beneficial power through spiritual laws such as unity, forgiveness, giving first fruits to God, speaking life, and walking in thanksgiving. "(Wisdom) cries out . . . 'Whoever is simple turn in here'" (Proverbs 9:3,4). Wisdom is this: understanding and walking in the laws of the spirit.

Declare: Like Solomon in II Chronicles 1, I cry out for the spirit of wisdom. I am now receiving revelation of the laws of the spirit that dramatically influence life. I release power to all around me as I allow these laws to work for me.

Checklist to Ignite Faith ___ BR, ___ RD, ___ DD, ___OD, ___ NF.

We don't wait for God to do something; but we, through wisdom (the laws of the spirit), increase and "grow" what we have been given.

Day #26
Valuing Joy
A merry heart does good like a medicine **(Prov 17:22)**

"Take three times a day for ten days and you will get better." When a doctor gives these instructions, most people are going to "obey." Why? They simply believe that it will work.

Our Great Physician has given us a prescription for health and strength; it is walking in joy. Dr. God says, "A merry heart is good medicine" (Proverbs 17:22) and "the joy of the Lord is your strength" (Nehemiah 8:10). Indeed the Bible teaches that joy is essential to a victorious life.

A main aspect of joy is laughter. Studies have proven the benefits of laughter. Cancer patients have been healed through a "prescription" of watching funny movies. Cells that destroy tumors and viruses increase through hearty laughter. "Energy-causing" endorphins are released into our body's system through hilarity.

Samson had a secret to his strength (Judges 13-16). The Philistines sought to discover this mystery. Like Samson, we too have been given a secret for strength. It's joy. Let's not forget it. It is the wise person who finds ways to increase the powerful prescriptions of joy and laughter.

Declare: I thank You, Father, that You are now giving me the keys to increase the "good medicine" in my life. By Your Holy Spirit I will purpose to "take" this powerful prescription every day so I can walk in health and strength for the great days of harvest ahead. Amen.

Checklist to Ignite Faith ___ BR, ___ RD, ___ DD, ___OD, ___ NF.

We must value joy as a fruit of the Spirit and
make it as much of a discipline and goal in
our lives as other fruits.

What About Job
What I feared has happened to me (Job 3:25)

Does Job's experience (read Job 1 & 2) teach us that God will send death, sickness, lack, and devastation into our lives to test our love for Him? Does He "allow it" and let the devil be His instrument of trials and testing? Or is there another answer to this question about Christian suffering? Our answer will greatly affect the level of victory that we have in life.

Here's what this writer believes. Job said, "What I greatly feared has come upon me" (Job 3:25). His fear gave Satan a legal access to "kill, steal, and destroy" from him. God "allowed" this attack only in the sense that He established spiritual laws (like the law of fear and the law of faith) that bring a result into our lives. Job's situation is similar to when Jesus told Peter, "Satan has asked for you, to sift you as wheat . . ." (Luke 22:31). Satan's eventual "sifting" of Peter resulted from a door of pride that Peter had opened. It was not a random attack, but manifested because of a violation of a spiritual law.

But, you might say, "We cannot take out the mystery of God. His ways are beyond human understanding." In response to this, I ask, "What then about God's promises? Are there any specific promises that we can truly believe (beyond eternal life and that 'all things work together for good')? Are His promises always secondary to His 'sovereignty'?" If we believe that, then it will be difficult to pray in faith again.

Declare: I live under a supernatural protection. I am shutting doors in my life to the enemy. I am opening doors for the blessing and power of God to flow in me and through me.

Checklist to Ignite Faith ___ BR, ___ RD, ___ DD, ___OD, ___ NF.

Day #28

What About Job (Part 2)

All that he (Job) has is in your (Satan's) power   Job 1:12

A traditional view concerning Job is this: God allowed Satan to ravage his life as a test of Job's character and love for God. This may sound plausible to some, but it is a teaching that leads to hopelessness and confusion about when we are to resist the devil.

We've already introduced Job 3:25 as the open door for Job's troubles – "what I have greatly feared has come on me." This fear is manifested in Job 1:4,5 where a worried and "stressed out" Job is continually offering sacrifices for his children. He was afraid that something bad was going to happen to them.

Look at verse twelve of chapter one. Notice what God said to Satan, "Behold, all that he has is in your power." This was not a handing over of Job to Satan, but a declaration of what was already true – because of Job's "open door" of fear. God did not put Job in Satan's hands. Job's fear put him in the hands of the enemy.

Is this difficult to accept? Maybe, but the alternative view is even more implausible – saying that God will use the devil to kill our family, destroy our property, and afflict our body. Again, if we accept this second view, then we are destined to never be able to pray in faith for specific areas of our lives, nor can we ever really be confident of God's will in our lives.

Declare: God is good and Satan is bad. Jesus came to destroy the works of the devil, not partner with him to accomplish God's purposes.

Checklist to Ignite Faith ___ BR, ___ RD, ___ DD, ___OD, ___ NF.

What About Job (Part 3)
The Lord gave and the Lord has taken away (Job 1:21)

What are we to infer from the above statement by Job? Does this mean that God can, and sometimes will, "take away" our family, our health, our finances, and our possessions as part of His plan for our lives?

We know God inspired all of scripture, but not every quote in the Bible are God's thoughts. For instance, the book of Ecclesiastes was written by a backslidden Solomon. God inspired this entire book to be in the Bible, but we cannot accept every conclusion from Solomon in Ecclesiastes as God's thoughts - because this writing is primarily an illustration of the cynicism and purposelessness that results from rejecting God.

Job's attitude of loving and blessing God during the toughest of times is powerful and is an example for us. We should not however allow Job's experience and conclusions to create our beliefs concerning the reason for negative things in life. If we accept a theology that "the Lord gives and the Lord takes away" in the areas of our health, protection, and loved ones; then there can be little faith in prayer. This would not be consistent with the message of the New Covenant.

Declare: Jesus has come to give me a "more abundant" life. The enemy is a thief seeking to steal, kill, and destroy (John 10:10). I resist him in Jesus' name.

Checklist to Ignite Faith ___ BR, ___ RD, ___ DD, ___OD, ___ NF.

Our conclusions about Job, or Paul's "thorn in the flesh", and other such areas will have much to do with our level of victory and influence for Christ.

Day #30
Judging The Faith of Others
Faith working through love (Galatians 5:6)

It is wise to use great caution when analyzing the faith of others. Here are three reasons why:

    1. We don't know how far they've come - We all start at different places. Some have inherited a place of great blessing by the faith of others. Others have practically started at "square one" in their faith walk. In God's eyes, someone could have "great faith", but seem weaker than many others. ("Man looks at the outward appearance, but the Lord looks at the heart" - I Samuel 16:7.)
    2. Corporate faith is more important than personal faith - Yes, individuals must take personal responsibility for their lives, but the local and regional church needs to be primarily concerned with possessing the "unity of the faith" (Eph. 4:12), which will increase the level of blessing and protection in its area of influence.
    3. Criticism and condemnation will actually decrease personal and corporate faith - Galatians 5:6 calls us to have "faith working through love." We need to look for ways to love and encourage people "where they are at" instead of being negative against seeming unbelief. Many people have become self-appointed "faith police officers" and have unwittingly caused hurt to others. Let's not be one of them.

Declare: The spirit of criticism is far from me. I am an encourager of the faith of others. I have great wisdom to know what to say (and what not to say) to those who are in a faith battle.

Checklist to Ignite Faith ___ BR, ___ RD, ___ DD, ___OD, ___ NF.

Day #31
Faith and Medicine
You will sustain him on his sick bed (Ps 41:3)

We have a big covenant with God (Hebrews 8:6). This "agreement" with Him includes a wonderful provision and promise for abundant health. Physical vitality is a major part of our benefit package (Psalms 103:2,3). Our faith needs to press in and receive what Jesus took stripes for (Is 53:3-4).

With this in mind, should a person of faith take any mediation? Is it permissible to consult doctors? Can we trust God to work through the medical profession or is this evidence of unbelief and putting our faith in man?

There are two extremes to avoid in this. The first is the reliance on man instead of God (Asa did this and was condemned - see 2 Chronicles 16:12). The other extreme is ignoring the fact that medicine ("take a little wine for your stomach's sake" - I Timothy 5:23) and doctors (i.e. Luke) are present in Scripture.

So what should we do? As an overcoming Christian, we should keep seeking to daily strengthen our faith. Like Abraham, we believe that next month and next year we will be able to receive more of God's promises in our lives. In the meantime, it can be wisdom (as part of our plan to strengthen our faith) to take medications and to benefit from the expertise of doctors. They will help us deal with symptoms in our physical bodies, as we keep pursuing being "fully convinced" (Romans 4:21) about our provision of abundant health for our lives.

Declare: I have wisdom concerning the use of medications and doctors.

Checklist to Ignite Faith ___ BR, ___ RD, ___ DD, ___OD, ___ NF.

Day #32

Wrestling for What
I will not let you go   (Genesis 32:26)

Jacob wrestled with the angel and made a tenacious dec-laration, "I will not let you go until you bless me." This "bull-dog boldness" got God's attention.

How would God choose to bless this person who would not take "no" for an answer? Money? A long life? A new camel? Victory over his enemies? A resolving of a difficult matter? No, his blessing was a revelation of his real name, his true identity. His name would no longer be Jacob, but it would be Israel (Prince With God). His blessing was this: he would receive a new sense of who he was - which would produce a change in his thoughts and vocabulary about himself. This, in turn, would cause a change in his actions and destiny.

The implications of this are revolutionary! One of the great-est things we can get from God is a new sense of who we really are. Once we call ourselves what God calls us, we will accelerate down the road of transformation.

We must move past just wanting God to fix our problems or to just have His blessing and anointing. We must get a hold of Him in our spirit and say, "I am not going to let You go until You bless with me with a true understanding of who I really am in You." Once this happens, everything changes.

Declare: I am a seeker of God. I go beyond simply wanting a situation changed. I seek God until He truly blesses me with transforming thoughts about my identity in Him.

Checklist to Ignite Faith ___ BR, ___ RD, ___ DD, ___OD, ___ NF.

Stop thinking of Christianity as a suppression of desire. We do not "repress"; we pursue a new identity by faith.

Day #33

Don't Withdraw Your Faith
. . . he will have whatever he says (Mark 11:23)

Here is a power truth for the victorious Christian: What we believe after we pray is just as important as what we believe when we pray. This principle is also true in ministry (what we believe after we minister is just as important as what we believe when we minister).

It is important to not withdraw faith after prayer or ministry. The devil wants us to curse the good seeds that have been sown by tempting us to speak unbelief concerning what has just been done. Certainly we can find areas where we can improve; but we must avoid negative, "concluding" statements that can undo much of the good that happened.

Jesus cursed the fig tree in Mark 11. The next morning "they saw the fig tree dried up from the roots." This tells us two things. First, our influence in prayer and ministry starts in the unseen (in the roots); thus, outward results (whether circumstances or feelings) should not be used to measure success or failure. Secondly, Jesus' **words** cursed the fig tree. We need to know that our words are powerful, and that they can bless or curse "spiritual seeds and trees" around us.

So what do we say after we pray or after we minister? The wise believer says, "I refuse to withdraw my faith. God did great things. His word will not return void" (Isaiah 55:11).

Declare: I thank God radically after I pray or minister. I refuse to curse through unbelieving declarations what has been done. I maintain and speak my faith; thus I see a greater harvest.

Checklist to Ignite Faith ___ BR, ___ RD, ___ DD, ___OD, ___ NF.

> Both God and Satan are after our words.

Day #34
Are We There Yet
I press toward the goal **(Phil 3:14)**

"Are we there yet?" Every parent has probably heard this question innumerable times. The usual answer is, "Not yet, but we are getting closer."

We know that we are "there" legally in possessing all of God's promises, but we also know that we are not experientially "there" in many areas of what is legally ours. This is an important distinction to understand.

The maturing person of faith can admit, "I am not there yet. I am experiencing such things as lack, sickness, confusion, failure, unsaved children, marital problems, and other "curses" because my life and faith have not developed to the place they will." Any other attitude creates hopelessness because we would believe we are victims and have no power concerning our future.

So let's keep moving forward in our faith. We personally may not completely get "there" in experiencing God's promises, but we can advance as far as we can so that our descendents (both spiritual and physical) can start at a better place than we did.

Declare: I will increasingly experience what is already legally mine. Lack is decreasing as my faith increases; and my faith is growing daily.

Checklist to Ignite Faith ___ BR, ___ RD, ___ DD, ___OD, ___ NF.

Like the men of faith of old, we will not see all
the promises manifest in our lifetime, but we will
make a difference for those who come after us.

Day #35
Escaping Into God
In His presence is fullness of joy **(Psalms 16:11)**

Our God is a refuge. How wonderful it is to regularly go into the secret place of His presence! We are transformed as we spend time with Him through worship, prayer, anointed ministry, and/or seeking Him with others.

Romans 15:13 says, "Now may the God of hope fill you with all joy and peace in believing." Even though we can be strongly touched in a meeting, we need to be more concerned with this question: what happens in us when the meeting ends or the music stops?

We need to escape into God and not simply escape from ourselves. It's possible to use the things of God as a diversion from our own need for personal healing. We may "hope" that the Spirit will do something; but without changing what we believe, it will only be short term. We cannot have a change in behavior without a change in the way we think.

What's the solution? Do we stop spending time in His presence? Of course not, but we need to expect a growing hope for our lives as a fruit of our times with Him. God's Spirit will loosen our spiritual soil so that the roots of hopelessness and unworthiness can be pulled out. Then we are truly escaping into God.

Declare: I love God's presence. He is my refuge and strength. Personal hope and joy are powerful fruits that comes from my "hiding place" times with God.

Checklist to Ignite Faith ___ BR, ___ RD, ___ DD, ___OD, ___ NF.

> Most people spend their life attempting to avoid pain, rather than attempting to live.

Day #36

The Goal: Being Fully Convinced
And being fully convinced . . . **(Romans 4:21)**

Abraham is the Bible's example of how to walk by faith. Even though he lived under the Old Covenant, he had a New Covenant revelation in regard to receiving from God. The victorious Christian must know what Abraham knew.

The Bible refers to different levels of faith. Jesus spoke of no faith, little faith, much faith, and great faith. Romans chapter four says that Abraham was "strengthened in faith" (vs. 20) and became "fully convinced that what He (God) had promised, He was able to perform" (vs. 21). Just as a weight lifter strengthens his muscles by pressing against resistance, the Christian can strengthen his faith through declaring God's Word and standing against negative looking circumstances. We can all move from no faith to the great faith of being fully convinced concerning God's promises.

"Fully convinced" is our goal. It is important to know where we are going. As with Abraham, we must embrace the process that leads to this full assurance. God's promises are not automatically possessed simply because we are a Christian. They are received by a "convinced" faith.

Declare: Like Abraham did, I am moving forward in my faith. I am strengthened today as I declare truth even in the face of seemingly dead circumstances. I am becoming "fully convinced."

Checklist to Ignite Faith ___ BR, ___ RD, ___ DD, ___OD, ___ NF.

> John 3:3 - "Unless you are born again, you cannot see the kingdom." We must exert our faith not only to receive Him as Savior, but to 'see' the kingdom at hand.

Day #37

Cause of Disasters
I will heal their land (2 Chronicles 7:14)

Hurricanes, floods, earthquakes, droughts, tornadoes, tsunamis, and other disasters happen around the earth. Are these random happenings that can occur anywhere and at any time? Are they God's "judgments"? Can we do anything to prevent them?

A disaster is an event that causes serious loss, destruction, hardship, unhappiness, or death. They did not exist on earth until Adam's rebellion – which set in motion earth's fury through natural disasters. There are none of these in heaven right now. They are a curse and not a blessing.

Scripture shows that calamities have spiritual "roots." In 2 Samuel 21 Israel was experiencing a prolonged drought. King David sought God and discovered the reason was his predecessor's mistreatment of a certain people group. He corrected the problem and the drought ended. This passage and many others clearly show that blessing and protection are influenced greatly by sin, righteousness, faith, and fear.

Are disasters then judgments by an angry God? Has He finally "had enough" and then punishes people? No. A better understanding comes through this thought: protection has been removed through continual violation of spiritual laws. God did not choose judgment, but we **chose** to live life apart from where He and His protection are. Remember, God's laws will work for us or against us. God's heart is not judgment (see Jonah), but He has allowed us to make our own choices that will influence the presence or absence of "natural" disasters.

Declare: Thank You God that others and I are humbling ourselves, turning from our wicked ways, and praying. As in David's day, thank You that You are forgiving our sin and healing our land (2 Chron 7:14).

Influencing the Economy, Weather and Public Health *If My people* (2 Chronicles 7:14)

Can believers positively affect climatic weather patterns, the economy, and the physical health of a nation? One well-known Bible verse gives us a clue. "If My people who are called by My name will humble themselves and pray and seek My face and turn from their wicked ways, then I will hear from heaven, forgive their sin, and heal their land" (2 Chronicles 7:14).

What does this healing consist of? If we look at verse thirteen of the same chapter, we see three areas of life to be "healed." God said, "When I shut up heaven and there is no rain (weather problems), or command the locusts to devour the land (economic difficulties) or send pestilence (plagues and health problems) . . ." After he listed these three problems, He says, "If My people . . ."

These negative circumstances are "sent by God" only in the sense that He has set up spiritual laws that, if followed, will bring blessing (and, if violated, will bring difficulties). He does not "choose" for these to happen, but man does by ignoring His principles. The amazing thing to understand though is that God's people have the ability to impact three vital areas of life: climate, economy, and health. Let's press into 2 Chronicles 7:14 and help reestablish God's protection in every area where we have influence.

Declare: I am humbling myself, praying, seeking God's face, and turning from my wicked ways. I am powerfully impacting my future and my nation's future.

Checklist to Ignite Faith ___ BR, ___ RD, ___ DD, ___OD, ___ NF.

Day #39
Attracting Favor or Rejection To Our Lives
As he thinks in his heart, so is he **(Proverbs 23:7)**

Do our beliefs make a difference in how others treat us? Are strife and rejection simply "bad luck" while favor and acceptance are "good luck"? The Bible indicates that there are spiritual laws that influence these matters. As we have said, wisdom teaches us to make these laws work for us and for the kingdom of God.

Luke 6:37-38 states the law of reciprocity. "Judge not and you will not be judged. Condemn not and you will not be condemned. Forgive and you will be forgiven. Give and it will be given to you . . . For with the same measure that you use, it will be measured back to you." Our inner attitudes and our outward actions cause a "giving" that brings an experience back to us (in proportion to the amount we have given).

We love others to the degree we love ourselves, thus our attitude toward ourselves becomes the basis for attitudes we "give" to other people. This, in turn, releases a harvest (an experience) in accordance with the measure that has been given.

Complicated? No. "As)a man) thinks in his heart, so is he." If a man thinks he is rejected, he is rejected. If a man thinks he is favored, he is favored. The key is to think about ourselves as God thinks about us (see 2 Corinthians 10:3-5).

Declare: God is good to me. I expect and receive His goodness. I give goodness to others in actions and attitudes. I therefore increasingly receive goodness and favor back in my relationships.

Checklist to Ignite Faith ___ BR, ___ RD, ___ DD, ___OD, ___ NF

Lasting favor comes not from what we do,
but from who we believe we are.

Day #40

Attracting Favor or Rejection To Our Lives (Part 2)
As he thinks in his heart, so is he (Proverbs 23:7)

Our beliefs make the difference in how others treat us. Indeed, strife and rejection are not simply "bad luck", nor is favor and acceptance the result from "good luck."

The Apostle Paul rebuked the Galatians by correcting a major doctrinal heresy that was blocking grace from their lives. They had moved from "faith based" Christianity to a "performance based" religion. One result of this "law emphasis" was "biting and devouring of one another" (Galatians 5:15). Their wrong beliefs about who they were in God actually attracted rejection and strife. They were cut off from grace (5:4), which blocked favor in relationships.

Those who have a "works doctrine" see themselves as rejected by God. This creates a performance environment where rejection and strife flourish. If we don't believe we have favor with God, how can we believe we could have favor with others? An unconscious thinking pattern will develop that believes mistreatment is deserved; thus, strife and rejection (biting and devouring) result.

On the contrary, those who believe they are radically favored (through Jesus) will have a positive expectancy of seeing His goodness in all aspects of life – including relationships. This belief will profoundly impact the increase of future "favor with God and man" (see Luke 2:52).

Declare: God supplies His Spirit and works miracles among us by the hearing of faith and not by the works of the law (Galatians 3:5). I believe the report of God's favor over my life. As Jesus did, I increase greatly in favor with both God and man.

Checklist to Ignite Faith ___ BR, ___ RD, ___ DD, ___OD, ___ NF.

Appendix One - Declarations

A note on these declarations: We won't have something just because we say something, but saying something is necessary to having it. If at the beginning of the 40 days, you don't understand fully why these three sets of declarations are important; then speak them by faith anyway. Some of the first devotionals will give clarity as to their importance.

Declarations List #1
These ten basic declarations (confessions) are foundational to the building of your faith. They will increase expectancy of God's goodness; and, thus, will increase the manifestation of that goodness in your life. Jesus said, "According to your faith, so be it" (Matthew 8:13). Say these (and the other declarations lists) every day for a month and see what happens to your life. It will be exciting! (Romans 4:17; Romans 10:9,10)

1. My prayers are powerful and effective (2 Cor 5:21; James 5:16b)
2. God richly supplies all my financial needs (Phil 4:19)
3. I am dead to sin and alive to obeying God (Romans 6:11).
4. I walk in ever-increasing health (Is 53:3-5; Ps 103:1-3)
5. I live under a supernatural protection (Ps 91).
6. I prosper in all my relationships (Luke 2:52)
7. I consistently bring God encounters to other people (Mark 16:17,18)
8. Through Jesus I am 100% loved and worthy to receive all of God's blessings (Gal 3:1-5).
9. Each of my family members is wonderfully blessed and radically loves Jesus (Acts 16:30.31)
10. I uproariously laugh when I hear a lie from the devil (Psalms 2:2-4).

Declarations #2

Remember this: Faith is the evidence of things not seen (Hebrews 11:1). Our "evidence" for things being true is not our circumstances, but God's promises. We don't deny negative facts in our lives, but we choose to focus on a higher reality, God's truth. Faith indeed comes by hearing (Romans 10:17); therefore, we choose to speak these powerful truths to build our own faith.

1. I set the course of my life today with my words (James 3:2-5).
2. I declare today that I cannot be defeated, discouraged, depressed or disappointed (Phil 4:13).
3. I am the head. I have insight. I have wisdom. I have ideas. I have authority (Deut 28:13; Deut 8:18; James 1:5-8; Luke 10:19).
4. As I speak God's promises, they come to pass. They stop all attacks, assaults, oppression, and fear from my life (2 Peter 1:2-4; Mark 11:23-24).
5. God is on my side today and therefore I cannot be defeated (Romans 8:37; Psalms 91).
6. I have the wisdom of God today. I will think the right thoughts, say the right words, and make the right decisions in every situation I face (1 Corinthians 2:16).
7. I choose life today. I choose health. I will not be depressed today. I will not be in lack today. I will not be confused today (Deut 30:19; Neh 8:10; Ps 103:1-3; 2 Tim 1:6,7).
8. I expect the best day of my life spiritually, emotionally, relationally, and financially in Jesus' name (Romans 15:13).

Acknowledgement: Many thanks to Gregory Dickow of changinglives.org for giving the basic outline for declaration lists #2 and #3.

Declarations #3

Truth: One of the main "methods" Jesus and the apostles used (in the gospels and Acts) was to SPEAK TO things. You will notice that they did not ask God to heal people, to cast out demons, or to raise the dead; but they spoke to bodies, to demons, to the wind, etc. Jesus encouraged us to speak to mountains in Mark 11:23. This set of declarations focuses much on our speaking to the various aspects in our lives.

1. I have a covenant with God and, by the blood of Jesus I release my divine protection and divine provision (Hebrews 8:6)
2. My angels are carrying out the Word of God on my behalf (Psalm 103:20)
3. I expect to have divine appointments today, to run into the right people, and to be delivered from the wrong people.
4. Any adversity, attack, accidents and tragedies that were headed my way are diverted right now in Jesus' name.
5. I speak to the raging waters in my life; peace, be still. I say to my mind; peace, be still. I say to my emotions; peace, be still. I say to my body; peace, be still. I say to my home; peace, be still. I say to my family; peace, be still.
6. Now I speak to every mountain of fear, every mountain of discouragement, every mountain of stress, every mountain of depression, every mountain of lack and insufficiency; and I say, "Be removed & cast into the sea in Jesus name!" (Mar 11:22-24)
7. And I speak to this day and I call you blessed. And I declare that I serve a mighty God who today will do exceedingly and abundantly beyond all that I can ask or think (Eph 3:20). I say you are a good God and I eagerly anticipate your goodness today.

Appendix Two - Negativity Fast

40 Day Negativity Fast
Igniting Faith in 40 Days

What a Negativity Fast is Not:
1. It is not denying that problems exist
2. It is not "stuffing things" that are wrong
3. It is not critical of others who may be struggling
4. It is not irresponsible concerning things that need to be done

What a Negativity Fast Is:
1. It is determining to focus more on God's promises than on problems
2. It is learning to speak with hope about even the toughest of issues
3. It is becoming "solution focused" rather than "problem focused"
4. It is refraining from react and giving voice to pessimism, criticism of others, self-criticism and other forms of unbelief
5. It is speaking about problems to the right people in the right way
6. It is replacing negative words & thoughts with positive words & thoughts based on the promises of God

Note: It is crucial to not only stop thinking and speaking unbelief and negativity; but to grow in thinking and speaking the positive: truth, the promises of God, praising God, encouragement to others and thanksgiving. The negative must be replaced with the positive in order for this fast to be effective.

Igniting Faith in 40 Days **has been used by many as a daily devotional book to read during a personal or group 40 day negativity fast.**

Appendix Three
Information on *Cracks in the Foundation*
A Book by Steve Backlund

From Its Introduction
A Paradigm Shift

The term paradigm shift was originally used to describe a change in basic assumptions within the ruling theory of science. It is also used to describe a major change in a thought pattern or a radical change in personal beliefs or organizations. It is a replacing of a former way of thinking with a radically different way of thinking.

When I read this definition (found in Wikipedia) of paradigm shift, I was struck by the phrase, "a change in basic assumptions." All of us have "basic assumptions" about God, others, the world and ourselves. These core beliefs result from our upbringing, our experiences and from religious teaching. They form a foundation for what we expect and subsequently experience in life. If we have the wrong assumptions, then we have "cracks in our foundation", and we will limit what can be built in us and through us.

This is a book that challenges many of the "basic assumptions" of familiar Bible verses and other common phrases. It is designed to help you think through what you believe. It has the potential to "fill" and repair many "cracks" in our thinking that rob us of potential. You may not agree with everything written, but I believe that you will be motivated to go to a higher level in "nailing down" your own beliefs about the key issues that are raised in "Cracks in the Foundation."

Why You Should Read *Cracks in the Foundation*

Steve Backlund is known for his wisdom and practical insights on "how to do life." The students in our ministry school - Bethel School of Supernatural Ministry - love him because he always leaves them encouraged and refreshed in their vision. He has an unusual gift to take the mundane and make it exciting, and to take the familiar and make it new. In his great book, Cracks in the Foundation, Steve goes beyond adding life to old thoughts; he successfully inspires the reader to take another look at common ideas that have gone unchallenged for far too long. In doing so, he builds a biblically based foundation of understanding that is very significant. In fact, I believe this foundation is necessary for us to fully embrace the reformation that is at hand. This is a book that I wish every Christian would read.

Bill Johnson
Bethel Church, Redding, CA
Author – *When Heaven Invades Earth* and other books

Sample #1 from *Cracks in Foundation*
We are living in the last days

Context: Matthew 24:42-44 is a passage that points us to a "last days" attitude. "Watch therefore, for you do not know what hour your Lord is coming. But know this, that if the master of the house had known what hour the thief would come, he would have watched and not allowed his house to be broken into. Therefore you also be ready, for the Son of Man is coming at an hour you do not expect."

Positive: Just as a person close to death is much more likely to concentrate on what is really important in life, there can be powerful motivation toward urgency and godly focus if we think that we have a limited amount of days left.

There will be a crack in our spiritual foundation if we allow a last day's emphasis to create fatalism in us about the future. This crack will grow wider if we unconsciously expect things to get worse around us in the end times (for our lives, our families, our communities, our nation and for the world). We will find that we are unable to believe God for revival in the nations of the world. Instead of believing and tenaciously claiming Psalms 2:8 for the people of the world ("Ask of me and I will give you the nations for your inheritance"), we will have uncertainty in our intercession. If the enemy can reduce our expectation of seeing people powerfully touched by Jesus (because, after all, it is the end times), then we have been duped into becoming spectators instead of "world changing" participants in life.

Conclusion: In describing the events of the day of Pentecost, Peter says, "But this is what was spoken by the prophet Joel: 'And it shall come to pass <u>in the last days</u>', says God, 'That I will pour out of My Spirit on all flesh . . .' " (Acts 2:17,18). Peter quotes Joel who said the events of Acts 2 were "end time events." We would do well to model our end time behavior and attitudes after the book of Acts (for they were in the last days too), not after those who would embrace a defensive or spectator mentality.

Sample #2 from Cracks in the Foundation
Every time I minister or move forward in God, Satan attacks me

Context: These words are frequently heard in churches and in prayer meetings. It is the apparent experience of many.

Positive: The devil hates Christians who are seeking to advance the kingdom of God. He is prowling around "like a roaring lion seeking whom he may devour" (I Peter 5:8). He especially wants to devour those who are moving forward in prayer, evangelism, leadership, and in obedience to God. It would be foolish for us to ignore the fact that we "wrestle not against flesh and blood, but against principalities, against powers, against the rulers of the darkness of this age . . . " (Eph 6:12).

There will be a crack in our spiritual foundation if we put more faith in Satan's power to attack us than in God's power to protect us. If we believe that the attacks of Satan (with its negative results) are normal, then our expectation of this will actually attract it to our lives (and will thus reinforce this lie as truth to us). Jesus said, "According to your faith, so be it" (Matthew 9:29). Those who believe they are protected will increasingly experience protection in their lives. Those who believe they will be attacked after moving forward in God (or in ministry) will increasingly have that experience in their lives.

Concluding Thoughts: Sometimes we overuse and overemphasize things like, "If the devil is not causing you problems, then you must not be any threat to him." There is some truth in this statement, but it too often creates a crack of believing that difficulty is the true sign of spirituality. Yes, the devil is looking for those he may devour, but he can only devour when there is agreement with him or fear of him. As people of hope and victory, we are to speak more about God's wonderful protection than we do about Satan's attacks and lies. As we do so, we will see that protection increase.

Find information about *Cracks in the Foundation* at Steve and Wendy's website: ignitedhope.com. Go there also for:

- CD teaching series that will inspire faith and hope
- Sermon downloads of recent messages
- Information on the Backlund's upcoming speaking itinerary
- Contacting Steve or Wendy about speaking to your church or group
- For many free helps to inspire your life